THIS BOOK
BELONGS TO:

Sonia Skakun
Love,
    Auntie Andrea

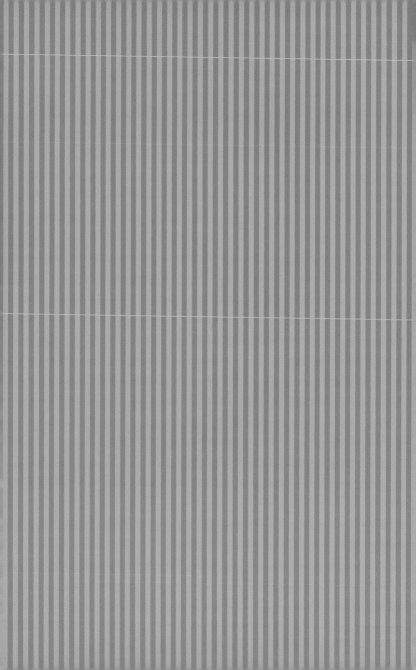

Unlikely Friendships

for Kids

Book One

The Monkey and the Dove
and Four Other True Stories of
Animal Friendships

by

JENNIFER S. HOLLAND

WORKMAN PUBLISHING
NEW YORK

For Kate, Will, Elliott, and Jasper.
And for Mom, of course.

Library of Congress Cataloging-in-Publication Data is available.

ISBN 978-0-7611-7011-2

Design by Raquel Jaramillo

Photo Credits: COVER: Front, CNImaging/Photoshot; INTERIOR:
p. 1, CNImaging/Photoshot; p. 4 © Sebastien Burel/Shutterstock;
p. 6 © Jennifer Hayes; p. 10 CNImaging/Photoshot; p. 12 © Zzvet/
Shutterstock; p. 14 © Tischenko Irina/Shutterstock; p. 18 © dpa/Landov;
p. 20 © Associated Press/Fritz Reiss; p. 21 Johannes Eisele/ddp/
Associated Press; p. 22–23 © EPA/Alexander Ruesche/Landov;
p. 26 Melanie Stetson Freeman/© 2006 *The Christian Science
Monitor*; p. 32, p. 37 © Deb and Terry Burns; p. 38 THE NATION/AFP/
Gettyimages; p. 40 © Media Union/Shutterstock; p. 42 © Anan
Kaewkhammul/Shutterstock

Workman books are available at special discounts when purchased in
bulk for premiums and sales promotions as well as for fund-raising or
educational use. Special editions or book excerpts can also be created
to specification. For details, contact the Special Sales Director at the
address below or send an e-mail to specialmarkets@workman.com.

Workman Publishing Company, Inc.
225 Varick Street
New York, NY 10014-4381

www.workman.com

Printed in the United States of America
First printing April 2012

Contents

A few years ago, I went scuba diving on Australia's Great Barrier Reef. This is a very special place in the ocean. Thousands of different types of fish live in or around the coral reef.

I noticed a puffer fish swimming near me.
The puffer fish was about the size of a softball.
He was alone.

The puffer fish did not seem to be afraid of me. I swam with him for a little while. He did not swim away.

I went back to the same area the next day. The puffer fish was there. This time, he was not alone. He was swimming with a school of fish called sweetlips.

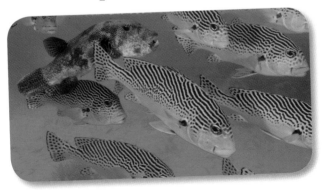

Sweetlips are very colorful fish. They have wide mouths, which is probably how they got their name. Sweetlips do not usually swim with puffer fish. But that is exactly what was happening. The sweetlips and the puffer fish were swimming together.

I went back again the next day. They were still together. What was going on? Why were they swimming together? I thought it was very interesting that two animals from different species

would be hanging around each
other like they were friends.
It made me wonder if other
animals became friends with
animals that were very
different from them.

I am a science writer. I write
about animals. So I decided to
write a book about animals of
different species who had
become friends. I had heard
some of these stories before.
The story of Owen and Mzee,
a tortoise and a hippopotamus
who became friends after

surviving a tsunami, was already famous. But I went looking for stories I had never heard before. I talked with people all around the world. I looked at many photographs. Sometimes the animal friendships were so unlikely that I wondered if they were true. But when I checked them out, they were!

Five of those stories are in this book. I hope you enjoy reading them as much as I enjoyed writing them!

—*Jennifer S. Holland*

Chapter One

The Monkey and the Dove

There is an island in China where hundreds of small monkeys live. These monkeys are called rhesus monkeys. Rhesus monkeys have many things in common with humans. Like us, they have strong bonds with their family members. Also, their families live together in groups, called *tribes,* which is similar to the way we live together in communities.

Mother rhesus monkeys take care of their young for a long time after they are born. They feed and protect their babies—just like human mothers do. They carry them wherever they go.

12

One day, some people found a baby rhesus monkey all by himself in the jungle. He was only about three months old—too young to be without his mother.

The people knew the little monkey could not take care of himself, so they took him to a nature reserve, a place where wild animals are protected by humans.

At first, the baby monkey was very scared. He did not

know where he was. But
he knew he was far away
from his home!

Then a wonderful
thing happened.
The baby rhesus
monkey met a
white dove that
was also
living on
the nature
reserve.

A white dove is often seen as a
symbol of peace and joy.

This white dove *did* bring peace and joy—to the baby rhesus monkey!

The baby rhesus monkey and the white dove became very close friends. At night, they slept together in the same cage. During the day, they both snacked on corn. The monkey would chatter at the dove, as if the dove could understand monkey talk. And the dove would coo at the monkey, as if the monkey could understand him.

Sometimes the baby monkey would pet the dove with his tiny hands. If only the dove had hands to hug him back!

In time, the baby monkey grew big enough to live on his own. He was taken back to the forest where he had lived.

At first, the rhesus monkey was afraid. But then he saw that his tribe was still living there. His tribe remembered him and welcomed him home!

The rhesus monkey started living in the jungle again.

The white dove was also released back into the wild. Even though they had become best friends for a while, both the rhesus monkey and the white dove were better off living in their natural environments. A monkey belongs in the forest. And a bird belongs in the sky.

Chapter Two

The Bear and the Cat

There was an old bear that lived in a zoo in Germany.
Her name was Mauschen.
She had lived in the zoo her whole life.

Mauschen was an Asian black bear. She was very shaggy.
Some people thought she looked like a giant black cat.

One day, a little black cat
appeared at the zoo.
No one knew where the
little black cat had come
from. The zookeepers
named the cat Muschi.

The black cat started
hanging around Mauschen.

Everywhere the bear went,
the cat followed. But the bear
did not seem to mind.

Mauschen liked her new little
buddy!

The two of them spent all
their time together.
They ate their meals together.
They slept next to each other.

People were amazed.
They came from all over the
world to see the bear and
the cat who were such good
friends. No one had ever seen
such a thing!

One time, the zoo needed
to make some repairs.
The zookeepers moved
Mauschen to a new room
that was inside a building.

But Muschi the cat did not
know what had happened
to her friend! She went all

around the zoo looking for
Mauschen.

Finally, when the repairs
were finished, the zookeepers
moved Mauschen back outside.

Muschi was so happy to
see her old friend again!
And Mauschen was so
happy to see Muschi, too!

To this day, no one can
explain why these two furry
black animals became such
good friends.

Chapter Three

The Elephant and the Dog

Tarra, an Asian elephant, spent many years performing for people all around the United States. When she grew older, she went to live in the Elephant Sanctuary in Tennessee. A sanctuary is a place where animals are sent to live a safe, happy life in the wild.

One day, a stray dog named Bella came to live at the Elephant Sanctuary, too.

Dogs and elephants have a lot in common. Dogs are friendly and very smart. So are elephants. Dogs are very loyal and have good memories. Elephants do, too.

So it might not seem surprising that Tarra the elephant and Bella the dog soon became buddies. They did everything together.

One day, though, Bella got very sick. She was taken to see a veterinarian. She had to stay indoors for many days until she got better.

During that time, Tarra was very sad without her little friend. She stayed outside the house that Bella was in. She never left the area. She was waiting for the dog to come out and play with her!

Luckily, Bella did get better and was allowed to go outside.

As soon as Tarra saw her friend, she ran over to greet her. She placed her trunk on her body to pet her. She stomped her feet with joy.

Bella wagged her tail and wiggled her body. She rolled on the ground to show how excited she was.

Like all good friends, Tarra and Bella were always there for each other, in good times and in bad.

Chapter Four

The Dog and the Cat

Dogs and cats aren't supposed to like each other. In cartoons and movies, dogs and cats are often seen as enemies. They chase each other. They scratch and bark. In real life, however, it is common to find dogs and cats living in the same home.

Libby, a tabby cat, was still just a little kitten when she went to live in the house where a dog named Cashew already lived.

Though Cashew and Libby didn't exactly "fight like cats and dogs," they didn't play together, either. They pretty much ignored each other—for twelve years!

But then, something happened that changed everything. Cashew started going blind.

It's not unusual for animals
to have trouble seeing when
they get old. What *is* unusual
is what Libby did about it.
The cat, who had never been
interested in the dog, suddenly
started to take care of him!

You hear about seeing-eye
dogs all the time, but who's
ever heard of a seeing-eye cat?
And that's exactly what Libby
became. She looked after
Cashew. She slept near him.
She would lead him to his
food bowl.

Sometimes the two of them would lie together in a sunny spot on the patio.

Everywhere the old dog went, Libby was there to guide him.

No one knows why Libby became Cashew's seeing-eye cat. No one knows whether Libby actually understood that Cashew could no longer see.

All that is clear is that Cashew was a very lucky dog to have such a loyal friend in Libby.

Chapter Five

The Lion and the Oryx

In the animal kingdom, all animals are either predators or prey. *Predators* are animals that hunt and eat other animals. *Prey* are the animals that get hunted by predators.

Lions are predators. They eat other animals for their food.

Lions hunt wildebeests, impalas, antelopes, and many other animals that live in Africa.

Eating other animals is a lion's natural instinct.

An animal's natural instinct is what makes it do certain things to survive.

One day, a young lioness that lived in Kenya did something that seemed to go against her natural instinct. The people in a nearby village who saw what this lioness did still talk about it—even though many years have passed.

The story has become a favorite all over the world.

What did the lioness do
that was so amazing?
The lioness had become
friends with a baby oryx!

An oryx is a type of African
antelope. It has two long
horns and black stripes.
Oryxes travel in herds for
protection against their
biggest predator: lions!

When the villagers first
saw the lioness with the
baby oryx, they thought she
was going to eat the oryx.

But after a few days, the villagers realized that the lioness was not going to hurt the little oryx. She was protecting the baby oryx as if he were her own baby. The lioness walked next to the baby oryx wherever he went. She even slept cuddled next to him at night!

The baby oryx began to think of the lioness as his mother. He tried to nurse from her. But the lioness had no milk to give the baby oryx.

The baby oryx began to
grow weak without milk
to drink.

In the wild, animals that
are too weak or too little do
not survive. The villagers
could tell that the baby oryx
did not have very long to live.

The villagers also worried
about the lioness. Since
she would not leave the oryx
to hunt for her own food,
she, too, was growing weak
with hunger.

Eventually, the oryx did die.
Humans get very sad when
someone dies, but no one
knows how the lioness felt
when the baby oryx died.
We do know that the lioness
went on a hunt the next day.
The food made her strong,
and she survived.

In the animal kingdom, there
are predators and prey—
except when the predator
becomes friends with its
prey. That may be the best
kind of unlikely friendship.

Animal List

 antelope: Deer-like mammal with horns. It lives in Africa and Southwest Asia.

 Asian black bear: Bear that lives in forests all over Asia. It is also called a *moon bear* because of a white, moon-shaped mark on its chest.

 Asian elephant: Elephant that lives in Southeast Asia. It is the second-largest land mammal. The African elephant is the largest.

 cat: Common house pet that is also an excellent hunter. Cats have been friends with humans for thousands of years.

 dog: Common house pet related to the gray wolf. Dogs have been friends with humans for thousands of years.

 dove: Bird that is found everywhere on Earth. A white dove is often seen as a symbol of peace.

 hippopotamus: Large mammal that lives in Africa and spends most of its time in the water. Its name comes from the Latin for "river horse."

impala: A kind of antelope that lives in southern and eastern Africa. It can jump a distance of 33 feet and as high as 10 feet.

 lion: Big cat that lives mostly in Africa. Lions are the only big cats that live in groups, which are called *prides*.

 oryx: A kind of antelope that lives in Africa. It has very long, thin horns that look like spears.

 puffer fish: Fish that can puff itself up into a ball with lots of spines to scare predators. It is also called a *blowfish*.

 rhesus monkey: Very smart monkey that lives in Asia. Rhesus monkeys are social animals and live in noisy groups called *troops*.

 sweetlips: Fish with large lips that often lives in coral reefs. Sweetlips are usually found alone or in small groups.

 tortoise: Reptile that lives on land and is protected by a hard shell. It is closely related to the turtle.

 wildebeest: Large African antelope with a short mane, a long tail, and horns that curve down and out. It is also called a *gnu*.

bond: A relationship that connects animals or people.

coral reef: A chain of underwater coral and limestone rocks near the surface of the ocean where fish and other sea creatures live.

herd: A group of animals that live and travel together; for example, oryxes travel in herds.

natural instinct: An automatic behavior that helps an animal survive.

nature reserve: A place where wild animals live under the protection of humans.

nurse: To drink milk from a mother's breast.

predator: An animal that hunts and eats other animals.

prey: An animal that gets hunted and eaten by other animals.

sanctuary: A place where animals are sent to live a safe, happy life in the wild.

scuba dive: To swim underwater using an oxygen tank and mask to breathe.

seeing-eye dog: A dog that has been trained to help blind people get around.

species: A group of animals of the same kind.

stray dog: A dog that has no home or owner.

symbol: Something that stands for something else.

tribe: A social group living together; for example, rhesus monkeys live in tribes.

tsunami: A big sea wave, caused by an earthquake or a volcanic eruption under the sea, that often leads to a flood.

veterinarian: An animal doctor, sometimes called a *vet* for short.

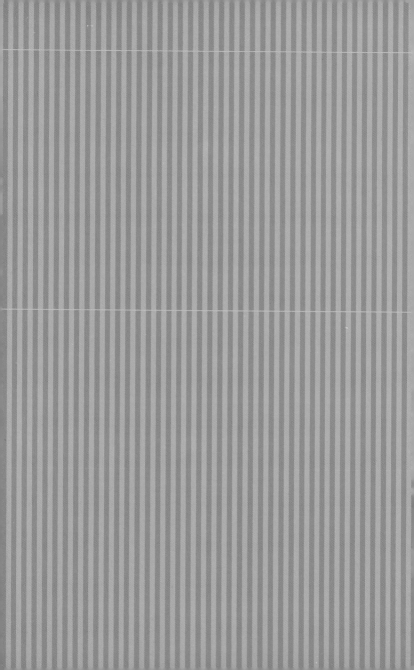